Why Am I a Slave?

Questions that have forever changed
our understanding of
the world

Titles in this series

Why Am I a Slave?

Questions that have forever changed
our understanding of
the world

A. Troglodyte, O.F.

COLLEGE PUBLICATIONS
LONDON

ISBN 978-1-84890-398-2

Published by College Publications
http://www.collegepublications.co.uk

———————————————————————————

Cover image: Frederick Douglass

Sapere aude[†]

Contents

Interview
with A. Troglodyte

by
Your Humble Servant

ৎৎ ৵৵

Some months ago, while digging for discarded literary treas-
ures in one of our local scroll shops, a friend and I chanced
upon several worn scripts credited to a certain A. Troglodyte.
Upon inquiry, we were told that the author had lived for
centuries (on this point the shop's proprietor obviously
misspoke, for surely he meant decades) in a cave on the edge
of the highland wilderness. Intrigued but unable to discover
much more than this, we packed up our provisions and headed
off in service to our London publishing house, deep into the
land of elves, trolls and troglodytes.

The journey turned out to be an arduous one, with the
winter frost upon us and many of the area's regular trails
having been washed out by seasonal floods. While fording one
stream we carelessly lost much of our gear, including all our
recording devices, with the result that the only report we are
able to give of our trip is one that has been reconstructed from
memory upon our return to civilization, a few days following
the events in question.

What we can say is that we did indeed eventually reach the
earthen home of one A. Troglodyte. We arrived in the early

afternoon, unannounced. Even so, we were welcomed without hesitation. Having been warned by some rather skittish townsfolk at the base of the mountain that troglodytes can be a grumpy lot when their meals are interrupted, we were determined not to infringe upon our host's dinner hour. What was on the menu I confess to having been too timid to ask. In his *Histories* (4.183), our friend Herodotus tells us that snakes, lizards and reptiles are the main staples of any troglodyte's diet. But, if so, I would hate to have seen the size of such creatures, judging by the enormous slabs of raw meat we saw marinating in the back yard.

In any event, we were soon asked to join our host, A. Troglodyte, for an afternoon of conversation and drinking. Half library and half cellar, the comfortable cave in which we found ourselves sat unobtrusively at the edge of the wilderness, far from the world's great centres of power but close to the quiet of the riverbank and the birdsong of the forest. When a neighbour happened to drop by to ask for a cup of gruel, we learned that our host was often referred to by friends simply as "Trog," although it was unclear whether this was the nickname of an individual or the kind of endearment that could be applied casually to any member of this hairy species.

Certainly, the visit was marked by generous hospitality, although in the darkness of the cave it was impossible to discover much about the shadowy figure who was our host. It came as a surprise – although perhaps it shouldn't have – that troglodytes as a species often devote much of the space within their cavernous homes to the storage of wine. Thus, over several bottles – troglodytes, apparently, do not use cups or glasses, but simply provide each guest with his or her own individual bottle – we learned quite a lot about the land we were visiting.

But about our host himself (or herself, or themselves – having never before encountered a member of this particular tribe, it was impossible for us to guess), we learned almost nothing. Even on the question of the authorship of the scrolls we had discovered, all we received was a short grunt, followed by a remark to the effect that the writing couldn't have been completed without the help of many friends. Later, our host did allow that careful readers should be able to learn all they wanted about scrolls such as *I Believe in Evidence* and *Some Quaint, Old-fashioned Advice* simply by reading them. Exactly what was meant by this remark was left unexplained.

What soon became clear is that, although troglodytes are often solitary, they are not hermit-like and regularly enjoy the company of family and even unannounced strangers. Certainly, they don't deserve the reputation they have for being fearsome and foreboding. They welcome visitors with enthusiasm and, although their dwelling spaces can appear somewhat cluttered, it soon became clear that only an illiterate rascal would confuse the peaceful tranquility of a troglodyte's cave with the noisy undercarriage of a troll's bridge, an observation we were eager to accept, not wanting to anger our otherwise accommodating host.

In our conversation, no topic was off limits. We discussed politics ("Machiavelli got it right, politicians can't seem to decide whether it's better to be feared or loved"), the un-seasonable weather ("There's a reason we study *average* temperatures"), advances in modern genetics ("As my children never tire of telling me: nature or nurture, it's still your parents' fault") and whether troglodytes are as old as they sometimes appear ("I did meet Methuselah once, although at the time I was obviously very young").

But what animated our host more than anything else was the new generation of young people, both humans and troglodytes, who had recently arrived at the local university. "What a remarkable group," Trog enthused. "It's an excep-tional generation, barely out of high school. But intelligent, hard-working and highly motivated. They're hungry for knowledge. And they're eager to learn as much as they can about the world they're about to inherit. They're certain to leave their mark. And it's up to us to help them."

Trog, it turns out, had spent many years both as a student and as an instructor at numerous universities on several continents. Now time was spent giving the occasional lecture at a nearby college.

"Passing on knowledge is harder than you might think," Trog told us. "There is always some new fad claiming to be of the greatest importance, some new trumpet call urging us to embrace an improved form of totalitarianism and some new skeptic telling us he knows for a fact that there is no knowledge and there are no facts. If there is one thing I've learned about teaching, it is that I can never enter a classroom without having someone join me who knows more than I do – Plato, Aristotle, Shakespeare, Locke, Newton, Douglass, Smith, Turing, Hemingway, Einstein – or at least their writings. Some ideas really are more important than others. Socrates got it right about the '-isms.' *Skepticism* about knowledge, *relativism* about truth and *nihilism* about values, they're all nothing more than an 'extremely tiresome bit of nonsense'" (*Theaetetus*, 162a).

"So, there's something distinctive and valuable about university life," I offered.

"More than anything, it's the idea that *knowledge matters*," Trog replied. That, and the intellectual enjoyment you can have there. It's the one place where you're given the time and resources to follow the evidence whether it might lead. Here in my cave, I can believe anything I want. But in the classroom, there's always someone challenging you, someone wanting you to explain why you believe what you do. In the classroom, I can still say anything I want. But I'd look pretty foolish if I couldn't back up what I say with evidence.

"So, this is what I tell my students: learning to read is important. This means more than just discovering the meanings of words. It means learning to retrieve sentiments that time and distance may have made obscure. It means discovering connections between words and a writer's thoughts. It means learning how to follow an argument. Reading is a skill that develops in parallel to learning. It requires attention and focus in a way that surfing the web doesn't. It means having the ability to climb inside someone else's head.

"Learning to write is also important. Good writing is easy to recognize. It's simply writing that makes readers want to read more. Being able to express your ideas in clear, understandable language gives you a tremendous advantage as you go through life.

"And before turning to a profession, it's important to learn something about both the arts and the sciences. Doing so teaches us the difference between creativity and discovery. It teaches us how to distinguish writing that helps us *know* from writing that helps us *feel*. It turns out that inquiry into even the most objective subjects can be helped by having a creative mind."

At this point our host took a book from a shelf and opened it.

"This is one of my favourite passages."

Then without another word, the book was closed and returned to its shelf. My companion and I both frowned.

"I can see you're curious. That's good. Curiosity about the world around us and about the people with whom we share it gives us the motivation we need to learn. And nothing helps us learn more efficiently than having the ability to ask questions. It's something young people are good at."

"So, you're optimistic about the future?"

"Of course."

"Troglodytes sometimes have a reputation for expecting the worst."

"It's not deserved. You can be a realist about the world and still be optimistic. I do admit that classics, philosophy, history and even the study of ancient and modern languages are now a little less popular than they once were. Not among young people, of course. But among university bureaucrats there's now a noticeable lack of interest."

"And this is something new?"

"There used to be a sort of gentleman's agreement about what the English physicist and novelist C.P. Snow called the university's two cultures. The humanities and the sciences were understood to be equally important. But they had different roles. The sciences were meant to advance knowledge. The arts and humanities were meant to be custodians of what has already been discovered and created, of what the Victorian poet Matthew Arnold called 'the best that has been thought and said.'

"Once discovered, scientific knowledge needs to be preserved, both in the library and in the classroom. But once created, works of art, literature and music not only need to be archived, they need to be experienced anew by each generation. The agreement was that if we never discovered a single new thing about Aristophanes or Milton or Shakespeare, or Mozart or Gershwin or Fitzgerald, this might be disappointing, but it wouldn't detract one bit from the benefits each generation gets from re-discovering their accomplishments.

"This meant there was an important distinction between the two main types of work done at a university. Some work is intended to *discover the new*. Other work is intended to *re-discover the old*. Neither is less or more important than the other. Mastering either requires curiosity and skill on the part of students and professors alike. The agreement was that within the university, there would be room for both. In some quarters, that agreement now seems to be forgotten. And that's a little sad."

"Do you blame the scientists?" I wondered.

"Not at all! They're good at what they do. They follow in the footsteps of Thales and Aristotle, and that's very much to their credit. But it's a shame that as a culture we also don't have the same enthusiasm about following in the footsteps of Solon and Socrates. 'Know thyself' and 'Everything in moderation': at one time these were more than just words carved into the stone walls at Delphi."

At this point the sun was getting low in the sky and the shadows in the cave were beginning to lengthen. Taking this as our cue to leave, we stood and thanked our host.

A few hours later when we reached our base camp, the mists had enveloped the mountain above us. The two of us began exchanging notes, just to be sure we were able to record as much detail about our visit as possible. But if anyone were ever to ask us how to return to the cave in which we had so pleasantly spent our afternoon, I'm sure that neither of us would be able to remember the path required to retrace our steps.

Having now returned to the warmth of our own hearth and submitted our recommendation to publish A. Troglodyte's various manuscripts to our employer, we do admit that it's good to be home.

Why Am I a Slave?

Homer	Why must we fight?
Plato	Why be moral?
Aristotle	What constitutes proof?
Leonardo da Vinci	Why is the sky blue?
Niccolò Machiavelli	Is it better to be loved or feared?
William Shakespeare	To be or not to be? That is the question
Galileo Galilei	Does the Earth move?
Thomas Hobbes	Why do we leave the state of nature?
John Locke	How do governments gain legitimacy?
Isaac Newton	Why does an apple fall?
Gottfried Leibniz	Why is there something rather than nothing?
Jean-Jacques Rousseau	Why is there inequality?
Adam Smith	Why does cooperation occur without coercion?
Heinrich Olbers	Why is the sky dark at night?
Thomas Malthus	Must population growth always exceed food supply?
Charles Darwin	How do new species arise?
Frederick Douglass	Why am I a slave?
Susan B. Anthony	Are women persons?
Gregor Mendel	Why are some traits dominant and some recessive?
Francis Guthrie	Can any map be coloured using just four colours?
Friedrich Nietzsche	Is God dead?
Georg Cantor	Is there just one size of infinity?
Sigmund Freud	Why do we dream?
Marie Curie	What causes radioactivity?
John Raskob	How high can we build?

Albert Einstein	What would it be like to travel at the speed of light?
Lester Pearson	How can there be peace?
Friedrich Hayek	Who plans best?
Margaret Mead	Is adolescence always an unhappy time?
Isaiah Berlin	Is it better to have *freedom from* or *freedom to*?
Alan Turing	Can machines think?
Arthur C. Clarke	Are we alone?
Nelson Mandela	Are human beings inherently evil?
Isaac Asimov	How can robots be made safe?
Martin Luther King, Jr	Where do we go from here?
Alice Munro	Who do you think you are?
Bob Dylan	What else can you do for anyone but inspire them?

Why Must We Fight?

Homer

But why must the Argives wage war against the Trojans?
Why has he gathered and led here an army, this son of
Atreus? Was it not for fair-haired Helen's sake? Do they then
alone of mortal men love their wives, these sons of Atreus?[1]

∾ ∾

The *Iliad* and the *Odyssey* are the oldest extant works of
Western literature. Often dated to around the 8th century BCE,
the *Iliad* tells the story of the final weeks of the Trojan War.
Led by Odysseus (the great king of Ithaca), and by Achilles
(the greatest of the Greek warriors), the people of the Greek
city of Argos (the Argives) and their allies battle to return the
beautiful Helen to her rightful home in Sparta. At the end of
the war, the *Odyssey* then relates the story of the ten-year
journey home of Odysseus (or Ulysses, as he was known later
to the Romans).

Since classical times the authorship of both epics has been
attributed to Homer, the legendary blind poet of antiquity.
Modern scholars debate the issue, with some still attributing
both books to Homer. Others believe that the two works were
composed gradually over several centuries and, hence, that
they lack a single author.

During the Hellenistic period, Homer was not only said to
have been struck blind by the shine of Achilles' armour, he
was also a common subject of cult worship, with more than

half a dozen cities claiming to be his birthplace. In Alexandria, Ptolemy IV Philopator – the fourth pharaoh of Ptolemaic Egypt – built a famous shrine to Homer. According to the 3rd-century Roman writer Aelian, in the shrine Ptolemy placed a statue of Homer and around it a circle containing all the cities "who laid claim to Homer."

Over the centuries, the *Iliad* and the *Odyssey* have inspired numerous other works of western literature, including not only Dante's *Inferno* and Cervantes' *Don Quixote*, but also more recent books such as Joseph Conrad's *Heart of Darkness*, James Joyce's *Ulysses* and Frank Baum's *The Wonderful Wizard of Oz*.

Part way through the *Iliad*, Odysseus does what he can to convince the sulking Achilles to leave his tent, telling him he is needed on the battlefield. In response, Achilles questions the importance of their continuing the war: "But why must the Argives wage war against the Trojans?"

"Why must we fight?" turns out to be a question people ask in every generation, in every war.

Why Be Moral?

Plato

Socrates, he said, do you want to seem to have persuaded us that it is better in every way to be just than unjust, or do you want truly to convince us of this?[2]

ഗ ള

The Greek philosopher Plato (428/427-348/347 BCE) writes often about questions of justice and morality. In his most famous book, *Republic*, he asks why people act morally. One answer is given by Plato's older brother, Glaucon. Glaucon suggests that the only reason people act justly or morally is to avoid punishment. In defending his suggestion, he tells the story of a shepherd named Gyges who finds a magic ring. By turning the wearer invisible, the ring allows even the most moral person to commit immoral acts without being caught. Upon discovering the ring's power, Gyges stops living a moral life. He murders his country's King, steals the affection of the dead King's queen, and becomes powerful and wealthy. Glaucon says that this is how we all would behave if we had the power to avoid punishment.

Plato's own view is harder to discover. Like a playwright, Plato hides backstage, letting only his characters speak. As a young man he seemed destined to enter Athenian politics. Legend has it that on his father's side, he had descended from one of the ancient kings of Athens, and perhaps even from the god Poseidon. On his mother's side, he was said to have been

7

a descendant of the great lawgiver Solon. But the fact that two of his relatives, Charmides and Critias, appear to have been part of the Thirty Tyrants, a group that briefly but brutally ruled Athens at the end of the Peloponnesian War, and the fact that the Athenians later executed his friend and mentor Socrates, appear to have soured him on the idea of participating in Athens' government.

Instead, Plato made multiple trips to Syracuse in the hope of turning the dissolute tyrant Dionysius II into a philosopher king. When their relationship soured, Dionysius had Plato placed under house arrest and sold into slavery. Luckily for Plato, a friend was able to purchase his freedom. When the friend refused Plato's offer of reimbursement, Plato used the money to purchase a piece of land outside the city walls of Athens. He then used the land to open his famous school, the Academy. Over the years, the school went through various changes of leadership, but it remained open some nine centuries before eventually being closed as part of the Christian Emperor Justinian's attempt to stamp out paganism.

Even so, throughout its history, the school never lost interest in many of Plato's questions, including the question discussed by Glaucon: Is it only the fear of being caught and punished that makes a person moral? Or are we moral for some other reason?

What Constitutes Proof?

Aristotle

Now a *deduction* is an argument in which, certain things being laid down, something other than these necessarily comes about through them. It is a *demonstration*, when the premisses from which the deduction starts are true and primitive, or are such that our knowledge of them has originally come through premisses which are primitive and true; and it is a *dialectical deduction* if it reasons from reputable opinions.[3]

ᔔ ᔕ

Aristotle (384-22 BCE) is the first Western thinker to create a fully comprehensive system of thought, a system that includes not just ethics and politics but also a detailed study of the natural world.

He is also the founder of formal logic, the discipline that tries to explain why some evidence rises to the level of proof while other evidence does not. He defines a *deduction* as an instance of reasoning in which a conclusion follows necessarily from its premises. He defines a *demonstration* (or perfect deduction) as a deduction from premises known to be true. In contrast, a *dialectical deduction* is a deduction based on premises that are only likely to be true.

Arriving at the Academy when he was seventeen, Aristotle studied with Plato for twenty years. Perhaps disappointed that he wasn't appointed Plato's successor as scholarch (or head) of the Academy when Plato died in 348/347 BCE – the position

9

went instead to Plato's nephew Speusippus – Aristotle returned to his hometown in northern Greece. There, he became tutor, not just to the future Alexander the Great, but to two other future kings as well: Ptolemy of Egypt and Cassander of Macedonia. Later, he returned to Athens where he established his own school, the Lyceum. Larger and wealthier than even the Academy, the Lyceum included the first known research library, a collection of writings used by everyone in the school and handed down to later generations of scholars to help them with their work.

Later in life, Aristotle and Alexander appear to have become estranged, likely for political reasons. Even so, when Alexander died, the rise of anti-Macedonian feelings in Athens led to charges of impiety being raised against Aristotle, something that motivated him to leave the city a second time. Recalling Socrates' earlier execution, Aristotle is reported to have said he was not going to allow the Athenians "to sin twice against philosophy."[4]

In the Muslim world, because of his creation of the discipline of logic and because of its use for diagnosing illness in the medical professions, Aristotle was remembered for centuries as "the first teacher." Because of his similar influence in Christian universities, he was known throughout Renaissance Europe as simply "the philosopher."

Why Is the Sky Blue?

Leonardo da Vinci

I say that the blue which is seen in the atmosphere is not its own colour, but is caused by the heated moisture having evaporated into the most minute imperceptible particles, which the beams of the solar rays attract and cause to seem luminous against the deep intense darkness of the region of fire that forms a covering above them.[5]

ᕦ ᕤ

Like Aristotle, Leonardo da Vinci (1452-1519) wrote about an amazing variety of subjects. Today, he is remembered, not just as a world-renowned painter and sculptor but as an important architect, engineer, mathematician, anatomist, botanist and inventor. The most famous of his scientific writings, the *Codex Leicester*, became the most expensive book ever purchased on the open market when it was bought by Bill Gates in 1994 for US$30.8 million.

Da Vinci's explanation of why the sky appears blue is not too far removed from the explanation still used today. As sunlight passes through the air molecules that make up our atmosphere, the energy from the light causes charged particles inside the molecules to oscillate. When this happens, the oscillation produces electromagnetic radiation that scatters the incoming sunlight in all directions, something now known as Rayleigh scattering. The Rayleigh Scattering Law states that the angle through which the photons are scattered varies inversely to the fourth power of the light's wavelength. As a result, blue light, which is at the shorter end of the visible spectrum, is scattered much more easily than, say, red light, which is at the longer end of the visible spectrum. This results in a clear, sunlit sky appearing blue since, when looking in any direction other than directly toward the Sun, the observer sees only scattered light.

Although Leonardo's parents were unmarried at the time he was born, Leonardo was still raised as his father's legitimate son. He began work as an artist's assistant at the age of fourteen, being introduced to a range of crafts including carpentry, metallurgy and drafting, as well as drawing and painting. Although probably gay, famously remarking that "the sexual act of coitus and the body parts employed for it are so repulsive, that were it not for the beauty of the faces and the adornment of the actors and the pent-up impulse, nature would lose the human species,"[6] it appears that he likely remained celibate for most of his life.

Some 500 years after da Vinci created them, his many mechanical and anatomical drawings remain the gold standard for these types of illustration. Debate also still rages over which of his paintings deserves to be the most famous: His *Salvator Mundi* (or *Savior of the World*) which sold in 2017 for a record-breaking US$450.3 million? His famous *Vitruvian Man* (c.1490) or *Self-portrait* (c.1490-1516)? Or his even more famous *Last Supper* (c.1495-98) or *Mona Lisa* (c.1503-19)?

As Sigmund Freud noted in reference to da Vinci's position at the beginning of the Renaissance, da Vinci "was like a man who awoke too early in the darkness, while the others were all still asleep."[7]

Is It Better To Be Loved or Feared?

Niccolò Machiavelli

From this arises the following question: whether it is better to
be loved than feared, or the reverse. The answer is that one
would like to be both the one and the other; but because it is
difficult to combine them, it is far better to be feared than
loved if you cannot be both.[8]

ço ೨

An Italian diplomat in the Florentine Republic, Niccolò
Machiavelli (1469-1527) is the first European writer in the
modern period to give a comprehensive, sustained theory of
political power. His book *The Prince* was originally published
under the title *De Principatibus* [*About Principalities*]. In it,
Machiavelli argues that it is better for a ruler to be feared than
to be loved. A ruler who is loved will retain his power only so
long as he is popular. A ruler who is feared will retain his
power regardless of circumstances.

Born in Florence at a time of political turmoil, Machiavelli
wrote comedies and poetry as well as books on political
theory. In the first decade of the 16th century while serving as
secretary to the Second Chancery of Florence, he was sent on a
diplomatic mission to Rome. Returning home, he became
further involved in politics, both as an observer and as a
participant. Thinking that citizens soldiers were likely to be
more effective in defending their homeland than mercenaries,
he began recruiting a Florentine militia. In 1509, he was

proven right when his citizen soldiers were successful in defeating the neighbouring city-state of Pisa. Perhaps in part because of his growing influence, he was arrested in 1513 after being accused of being involved in a conspiracy to force the Medici family from power. He denied his involvement and was released after three weeks of imprisonment and torture.

Machiavelli's book *Discourses on Livy* focuses nominally on the history of the Roman Empire, but the book often uses Roman historical episodes merely as examples to illustrate the author's underlying political philosophy. Like hundreds of other books, both *The Prince* and the *Discourses* were eventually placed on the Catholic Church's *Index of Prohibited Books*.

Because Machiavelli believed rulers are justified in using force to eliminate their rivals and deceit to achieve their political goals, he is also famous for his claim that the ends justify the means. Perhaps it is not surprising that Machiavelli himself is still remembered with the disparaging adjective "Machiavellian."

To Be or Not To Be?
That Is the Question

William Shakespeare

To be, or not to be? That is the question:
Whether 'tis nobler in the mind to suffer
The slings and arrows of outrageous fortune,
Or to take arms against a sea of troubles,
And by opposing end them? To die: to sleep;
No more; and by a sleep to say we end
The heart-ache and the thousand natural shocks
That flesh is heir to, 'tis a consummation
Devoutly to be wish'd. To die, to sleep;
To sleep: perchance to dream: ay, there's the rub;
For in that sleep of death, what dreams may come
When we have shuffled off this mortal coil,
Must give us pause …[9]

ço ɔ

During his lifetime, William Shakespeare (1564-1616) was a member and part owner of one of London's most successful theatrical companies, the Lord Chamberlain's Men. Today he is credited with being England's greatest poet and dramatist.

Set in Denmark, his *Hamlet* tells the story of how a young prince plans revenge against his uncle Claudius, the man who has murdered his father, married his mother and seized his father's throne. The play is often said to be among the most philosophical of Shakespeare's writings. When speaking to his friend Rosencrantz, Hamlet comments that "there is nothing either good or bad, but thinking makes it so,"[10] raising the question of subjectivism in ethics. In his famous monologue "What a piece of work is man,"[11] he comments skeptically on the human condition, and with his question "To be or not to be?" he ponders the very meaning of life itself.

By one estimate, Shakespeare introduced – or at least made the first recorded use of – some 2,035 new words.[12] He wrote hundreds of poems and at least thirty-seven plays. It is often said that he died on his birthday (April 23), although scholars are more certain about his death date than his birth date. He is buried next to his wife, Anne Hathaway, in a shallow grave in Stratford-Upon-Avon, his hometown. On his grave stones, written in the spelling of Shakespeare's time, are the words,

> Good frend for Jesus sake forbeare,
> To digg the dust enclosed heare.
> Bleste be ye man that spares thes stones,
> And curst be he that moves my bones.[13]

In 2016, archaeologists were able to use ground-penetrating radar to confirm that although Shakespeare's remains are still there, it appears likely that his skull may have been stolen by grave robbers. Today many of the twenty-seven known moons of Uranus are named after Shakespearean characters.

In the 1623 posthumous collection of Shakespeare's plays known as the *First Folio*, Shakespeare's fellow playwright and poet Ben Jonson wrote famously that Shakespeare and his writings were "not of an age, but for all time."[14] It is a generous judgment that has only grown in authority over the centuries.

Does the Earth Move?

Galileo Galilei

I, Galileo, son of the late Vincenzio Galilei of Florence, seventy years of age, arraigned personally for judgment, kneeling before you Most Eminent and Most Reverend Cardinals Inquisitors-General against heretical depravity in all of Christendom, having before my eyes and touching with my hands the Holy Gospels, swear that I have always believed, I believe now, and with God's help I will believe in the future all that the Holy Catholic and Apostolic Church holds, preaches, and teaches. However, whereas, after having been judicially instructed with injunction by the Holy Office to abandon completely the false opinion that the sun is the center of the world and does not move and the earth is not the center of the world and moves, and not to hold, defend, or teach this false doctrine in any way whatever, orally or in writing; and after having been notified that this doctrine is contrary to Holy Scripture; I wrote and published a book in which I treat of this already condemned doctrine and adduce very effective reasons in its favor, without refuting them in any way; therefore, I have been judged vehemently suspected of heresy, namely of having held and believed that the sun is the center of the world and motionless and the earth is not the center and moves.

Therefore, desiring to remove from the minds of Your Eminences and every faithful Christian this vehement suspicion, rightly conceived against me, with a sincere heart and unfeigned faith, I abjure, curse, and detest the above-mentioned errors and heresies, and in general each and every other error, heresy, and sect contrary to the Holy Catholic Church ... [15]

17

Because of his ground-breaking work in mechanics, astronomy and mathematics, Galileo Galilei (1564-1642) is often referred to as the "father of modern science." Famously, his advocacy of Copernicanism – the theory that the Earth orbits around the Sun – ran counter to the geo-centrism of the Catholic Church. As a result, Galileo was called to appear before the Inquisition, found "vehemently suspect of heresy," and threatened with torture if he refused to recant. (It probably didn't help that in his most famous book, *Dialogue Concerning Two Chief World Systems* published in 1632, he named the character advocating the pope's view "Simplicio.") After recanting, legend has it that as Galileo rose from kneeling before his inquisitors, he murmured, "*e pur, si muove* [even so, it moves]." Because of what he had written, he spent the rest of his life under house arrest.

Over a century later in 1757, Galileo's *Two Chief World Systems* was finally removed from the Church's *Index of Prohibited Books*. Even so, it wasn't until 1992, three years after Galileo's namesake spacecraft had been launched on its way to Jupiter, that the Vatican issued a half-hearted statement finally closing its file on Galileo. No apology was issued for the arrest or the threatened torture. Instead, it was merely noted that in the case of Galileo there was "A tragic mutual misunderstanding" and that "often, beyond two partial and contrasting visions, there is a broader vision that includes and surpasses them both."[16]

Why Do We Leave the State of Nature?

Thomas Hobbes

Hereby it is manifest, that during the time men live without a common Power to keep them all in awe, they are in that condition which is called War ... where every man is Enemy to every man ... In such condition, there is no place for Industry; because the fruit thereof is uncertain; and consequently no Culture of the Earth; no Navigation, nor use of the commodities that may be imported by Sea; no commodious Building; no Instruments of moving, and removing such things as require much force; no Knowledge of the face of the Earth; no account of Time; no Arts; no Letters; no Society; and which is worst of all, continuall feare, and danger of violent death; And the life of man, solitary, poor, nasty, brutish, and short.[17]

ೀ ೀ

The first modern advocate of what is now called *social contract theory*, Thomas Hobbes (1588-1679) argued in favour of self-interested cooperation and the importance of having a strong leader (or leviathan) to enforce the rule of law. Many commentators have remarked that Hobbes' rather pessimistic description of life without government – which he called the *state of nature* – may have resulted from the fact that he lived during some of the harshest times in European history, including the bloody English civil war. After being born prematurely, supposedly because his mother was worried about the imminent invasion of the Spanish Armada, Hobbes and his family were abandoned by his clergyman father who had been caught brawling in his parish churchyard. As Hobbes reported, "my mother gave birth to twins: myself and fear."[18] Despite such unpromising beginnings, Hobbes somehow managed to get himself admitted to Oxford by the time he was fourteen.

Hobbes believed that without strong government, a state of war – in which no one was restrained from having "dominion over others" – would be inevitable.[19] It is for this reason that people voluntarily agree to give up some of their freedoms to live in a commonwealth in which the laws protect, not just the strongest among us, but everyone equally. The result, says Hobbes, is "a more contented life" in which the "miserable condition of War" can be avoided.[20]

Even so, after publishing his *Elements of Law* in 1640, Hobbes found it necessary to flee to Paris. Both the Catholic Church and the University of Oxford had begun to ban his books and, perhaps more worrisome, there was even some talk of burning Hobbes himself! Eventually he returned to England and after Charles II was returned to the throne, the king granted him a pension of £100 a year.

Years later in 1666, when the House of Commons began preparing a bill against atheism, Hobbes himself burned many of his papers, worried that they might fall into the wrong hands. He died in 1679 after suffering a stroke. On his tombstone are the words, "He was a virtuous man, and for his reputation for learning, he was well known at home and abroad." Legend has it that Hobbes had preferred just the slogan, "This is the true philosopher's stone."[21]

How Do Governments Gain Legitimacy?

John Locke

Who shall judge whether the prince or legislature act contrary
to their trust? ... To this I reply: The people shall be judge.[22]

ॐ ॐ

Trained at Oxford in both philosophy and medicine, John
Locke (1632-1704) famously argued against both Robert
Filmer's theory of the divine right of kings and Thomas
Hobbes' theory of absolute government. In contrast to these
two views, Locke held that governments obtained their
legitimacy only through the consent of the governed. Sometimes referred to as the "father of liberalism," he is widely
regarded as one of the most influential Enlightenment thinkers
of the 17th century.

In epistemology – or the theory of knowledge – Locke
abandoned René Descartes' idea that knowledge is based on
pre-existing concepts and instead championed what was then a
radical form of empiricism, postulating that at birth the mind is
a blank slate (or *tabula rasa*) and that all human knowledge
arises through experience. In politics, he argued that
sovereignty resides in the citizenry and that it is only through
voluntary social contracts and a respect for natural rights that
legitimate governments are born. In his *Letter Concerning
Toleration*, he is also famous for his defence of the separation
of Church and State. Nowhere is his influence more apparent

than in many of the founding documents of the United States, including the 1776 *Declaration of Independence*.

Despite such influence, Locke's theory of slavery has famously diminished his reputation as a champion of individual liberty. According to Locke, there sometimes can be a moral justification of slavery. Such a justification is provided by a just-war theory in which an unjust aggressor is defeated in war and the victor then elects to enslave rather than execute his enemies. In this sense, a state of slavery is the continuation of the state of war between a lawful conqueror and a captive. It is a justification that many people believe is far too easily open to abuse and that represents a clear moral failing on Locke's part.

Twice, Locke found it prudent to leave England for political reasons. The first was when his patron, the 1st Earl of Shaftesbury, fell from political favour. As a result, Locke spent several years travelling in France. The second was when he fled to the Netherlands, having been unjustly accused of being involved in the Rye House Plot, a plan to assassinate King Charles II and his brother, the Duke of York. Locke returned to England only after the Glorious Revolution of 1688 and the replacement of the Catholic King James with his Protestant daughter Mary. He died three years before the *Acts of Union* took place in 1707, completing the political union of England and Scotland. Having helped lay the groundwork for the modern, constitutional monarchy that would eventually become the United Kingdom of Great Britain and Northern Ireland, Locke died, famous for his sincerity and for his comment that "Whatever I write, as soon as I discover it not to be true, my hand shall be the forwardest to throw it into the fire."[23]

Why Does an Apple Fall?

Isaac Newton

The weather being warm, we went into the garden and drank tea, under shade of some apple-trees, only he and myself. Amidst other discourses, he told me, he was just in the same situation, as when formerly, the notion of gravitation came into his mind. It was occasioned by the fall of an apple, as he sat in contemplative mood. Why should that apple always descend perpendicularly to the ground, thought he to himself. Why should it not go sideways or upwards, but constantly to the earth's centre.[24]

Born the same year Galileo died, Isaac Newton (1642-1727) was one of the most influential figures of the 17th century. His book *Philosophiae Naturalis Principia Mathematica* (or *Mathematical Principles of Natural Philosophy*) introduced, not just a universal theory of gravitation but the entire system of mathematics on which classical mechanics is based. It was from his laws of motion that he was able to derive Kepler's laws of planetary movement, the movement of tides and the trajectories of comets. His work in optics not only allowed him to show how white light can be divided into all the colours of the visible spectrum, it also helped him construct one of the first reliable reflecting telescopes. Often remembered as one of the inventors of the differential and integral calculus, Newton is also regularly recognized as one of the greatest mathematicians in history.

As a student at Trinity College, Cambridge, Newton began his studies as a subsizar, working in the college in return for room and board. Later, he was awarded a university scholarship. Following the Great Plague – during which the university was temporarily closed – he returned to Cambridge and was elected a Fellow at Trinity, whose other Fellows have included not just Francis Bacon, Charles Babbage and G.H. Hardy, but also Bertrand Russell, Ludwig Wittgenstein, Alfred Tennyson and Amartya Sen.

Famously, Newton wrote,

> I do not know what I may appear to the world; but to myself I seem to have been only like a boy playing on the seashore, and diverting myself in now and then finding a smoother pebble or a prettier shell than ordinary, whilst the great ocean of truth lay all undiscovered before me.[25]

Toward the end of his career, he served as president of the Royal Society and twice as Member of Parliament for the University of Cambridge. He was knighted by Queen Anne in 1705.

Why Is There Something
Rather Than Nothing?

Gottfried Leibniz

The first question we have the right to ask will be, why is there something rather than nothing? For nothing is simpler and easier than something. Furthermore, assuming that things must exist, we must be able to give a reason for why they must exist in this way, and not otherwise.[26]

ço ço

Gottfried Wilhelm Leibniz (1646-1716) is remembered as one of Europe's last great renaissance men – a scholar who mastered and contributed to virtually every known branch of knowledge, including fields as diverse as biology, psychology, probability theory, philology, ethics and law. Independently of Newton, Leibniz also invented his own version of the infinitesimal calculus, a version that is in some ways more like the one most people use today. He also created some of the theory underlying the future invention of mechanical calculators, developing a calculator that could not only add and multiply numbers – similar to the calculator invented by Blaise Pascal half a century earlier – but that could also multiply, divide and extract roots.

In 1714, Leibniz asked the question, "Why is there something rather than nothing?" Believing that "nothing takes place without sufficient reason,"[27] he concluded that the existence of the physical universe shows there has to be an all-knowing, all-powerful, supernatural creator. What's more, the only world such a creator could create would have to be the best of all possible worlds.

In response to the idea that we are living in the best of all possible worlds, Leibniz was ridiculed mercilessly by Voltaire. In his novella *Candide*, Voltaire reminds his readers, not only about the theoretical problem of living in an imperfect world created by a perfect God but about many real-life historical hardships, including the Seven Years' War and the 1755 Lisbon earthquake. In every such case, the worried Candide character is reassured by the ridiculously optimistic Professor Pangloss that "all is for the best" in the "best of all possible worlds."[28] In response to the need for a supernatural creator, Voltaire also points out that if literally everything needs to have a creator, then surely even a creator would need to have a creator.

Upon his death, Leibniz was buried in a grave that remained unmarked for half a century. In 1985, the German government created the Leibniz Prize, one of the richest prizes in the world for exceptional scientific and academic work.

Why Is There Inequality?

Jean-Jacques Rousseau

Man is born free, and everywhere he is in chains. He who believes himself the master of others does not escape being more of a slave than they. How did this change take place? I have no idea. What can render it legitimate? I believe I can answer this question.[29]

ॐ ॐ

Jean-Jacques Rousseau (1712-78) wrote two of his most famous essays in response to questions asked by the French Academy of Dijon as part of its annual essay competition. In 1750, the Academy asked "whether the re-establishment of the sciences and the arts contributed to purifying morals."[30] Rousseau won the competition by arguing in his *Discourse on the Arts and Sciences* that it did not. Six years later, he wrote in answer to the question, "What is the origin of inequality among men, and is it authorized by natural law?"[31] This time, his *Discourse on the Origin and Basis of Inequality among Men* failed to win. He later expanded the essay into his book, *The Social Contract*.

Rousseau's answer to the question of why there is inequality is a simple one: It is the result, he says, not of nature but of social convention. As he explains it, "the social order is a sacred right which serves as a foundation for all other rights. Nevertheless, this right does not come from nature. It is therefore founded upon convention."[32]

Even so, Rousseau's suggestion that we can enter into social organizations governed by "a general will" while at the same time retaining our individual liberty has seemed to many commentators to be a less-than-plausible suggestion. Not only does Rousseau emphasize that governments need to protect citizens' collective (rather than individual) interests. He also concludes that people who are unable to recognize their own best interests will need to be forced to adapt to the general will of their county's leaders. In Rousseau's romantic but perhaps misleading phrase, they will "be forced to be free."[33]

So great was Rousseau's reputation that when he died he was buried in the Paris Panthéon next to Voltaire.

Why Does Cooperation Occur without Coercion?

Adam Smith

> It is not from the benevolence of the butcher, the brewer, or the baker, that we expect our dinner, but from their regard to their own interest. We address ourselves, not to their humanity but to their self-love, and never talk to them of our own necessities but of their advantages.[34]

♏ ♏

Adam Smith (1723-90) published his landmark work *An Inquiry into the Nature and Causes of the Wealth of Nations* (usually shortened to *The Wealth of Nations*) in 1776, the same year the American *Declaration of Independence* was signed and the same year his friend David Hume died. He is generally regarded as the founder of both modern economic theory and modern political economy.

In response to the question of why cooperation occurs without coercion, Smith observes that cooperation often occurs simply as the result of good will between neighbours. But even more often, it is the result of mutual benefit:

> Man has almost constant occasion for the help of his brethren, and it is in vain for him to expect it from their benevolence only. He will be more likely to prevail if he can interest their self-love in his favour, and show them that it is for their own advantage to do for him what he requires of them. Whoever

offers to another a bargain of any kind, proposes to do this. Give me that which I want, and you shall have this which you want, is the meaning of every such offer; and it is in this manner that we obtain from one another the far greater part of those good offices which we stand in need of.[35]

After entering the University of Glasgow at age fourteen, Smith moved to Oxford University in 1740. In 1748, he gave a series of public lectures at the University of Edinburgh where he met and became friends with Hume. He returned to the University of Glasgow as a faculty member in 1751. In 1759, Smith published *The Theory of Moral Sentiments*, arguing that human morality depends primarily on the sympathy that people have for one another.

Given Smith's reluctance to sit for a portrait, all paintings of Smith except one appear to have been painted from memory. As Smith commented, "I am a beau in nothing but my books."[36]

In 2007, the asteroid 12838-AdamSmith was named after him. The same year, he became the first Scotsman to be featured on an English banknote.

Why Is the Sky Dark at Night?

Heinrich Olbers

> If there really are suns throughout the whole of infinite space,
> and if they are placed at equal distances from one another, or
> grouped into systems like that of the Milky Way, their
> number must be infinite and the whole vault of heaven must
> appear as bright as the Sun … It goes without saying that
> experience contradicts this argument.[37]

ço ez

A medical doctor who specialized in the new study of
ophthalmology and who studied astronomy in his spare time,
Heinrich Olbers (1758-1840) installed an observatory on the
second floor of his house, using its two large bay windows to
position his telescopes. Using them, he discovered the
asteroids (or what were then called the "minor planets") Pallas
and Vesta, as well as several comets. He also took a leading
role in the hunt for a planet between Mars and Jupiter and,
together with the mathematician Carl Gauss, he worked to
discover the orbit of the asteroid Ceres, the first asteroid
discovered in the modern period. Olbers also devised a
method, still used today, for calculating a comet's orbit and he
remains famous for drawing people's attention to the question
of why we see so few stars at night.

Since there are so many trillions of stars, why don't they
illuminate the night sky more brightly? Why doesn't their
combined light completely fill the night sky? If the only thing

blocking our view of a distant star is another, closer star, shouldn't the sky at night be just as bright as during the day? It is a puzzle that wasn't solved until near the end of the 20th century when it was realized that the main reason the sky is dark at night is that galaxies have finite age. This means that the amount of light that stars have been pumping into empty space turns out to be finite, since it is restricted by the age of each star and the time it takes for light from distant galaxies to reach the Earth. In other words, even if the universe turns out to be significantly larger than what we can directly observe, we still will be able to see sources of radiation from only a limited volume of space.

Must Population Growth
Always Exceed Food Supply?

Thomas Malthus

Must it not then be acknowledged by an attentive examiner of the histories of mankind, that in every age and in every State in which man has existed, or does now exist: That the increase of population is necessarily limited by the means of subsistence?[38]

ঌ ঌ

According to his biographer, because of his views about population growth, Thomas Malthus (1766-1834) was "the best-abused man of the age ... Here was a man who defended small-pox, slavery, and child-murder; who denounced soup-kitchens, early marriage, and parish allowances ... ."[39]

Widely misinterpreted as defending the most harmful atrocities and as forecasting some great future disaster, Malthus actually argued that the many miseries human beings currently suffer (starvation, disease, war and other cruelties) are the inevitable consequences of imbalances resulting from the limited means of subsistence (food and other necessities) along with the constant natural pressure of increased population growth.

According to Malthus, population growth always works to exceed food supply. As a result, the limit of food supply

implies a strong and constantly operating check on population
... This difficulty must fall somewhere and must necessarily be
severely felt by a large portion of mankind.[40]

In short, "the superior power of population cannot be checked
without producing misery or vice," and "the ample portion of
these two bitter ingredients in the cup of human life and the
continuance of the physical causes that seem to have produced
them bear too convincing a testimony."[41]

A professor of history and political economy at the East
India Company College, Malthus was elected to the Royal
Society in London, the Royal Academy in Berlin and the
Académie des Sciences Morales et Politiques in Paris. A friend
of both the economist David Ricardo and the philosopher
James Mill, Malthus became one of the co-founders of the
Statistical Society of London in 1834.

How Do New Species Arise?

Charles Darwin

Again, it may be asked, how is it that varieties, which I have called incipient species, become ultimately converted into good and distinct species, which in most cases obviously differ from each other far more than do the varieties of the same species? How do those groups of species, which constitute what are called distinct genera, and which differ from each other more than do the species of the same genus, arise?[42]

ᔅ ᔃ

The most famous advocate of a wholly natural theory of evolution, Charles Darwin (1809-82) argued that random variation leads to differences being transmitted to subsequent generations of a species. Organisms better adapted to their environment then tend to survive longer and to produce more offspring. As Darwin writes, because of the struggle for life,

> any variation, however slight and from whatever cause proceeding, if it be in any degree profitable to an individual of any species, in its infinitely complex relations to other organic beings and to external nature, will tend to the preservation of that individual, and will generally be inherited by its offspring.[43]

It follows that offspring will then have a better chance of surviving and eventually a new species will result.

Darwin called his key insight the Principle of Natural Selection. It is a principle that has been as widely and as successfully confirmed as almost any other scientific principle in human history. Almost as famous as his 1859 book *On the Origin of Species by Means of Natural Selection*, his 1871 book *The Descent of Man, and Selection in Relation to Sex* applies Darwin's theory of evolution to human populations. In it, Darwin describes his theory of sexual selection, a form of biological adaptation similar to, but distinct from, natural selection.

Born on the same day as Abraham Lincoln, Darwin entered the University of Edinburgh at age sixteen. He then famously travelled around the world for five years on board the HMS Beagle. Darwin's field notes from this voyage formed the basis of his 1839 book, *Journal and Remarks*. The book's popularity encouraged the publisher to re-issue it later that same year as *Darwin's Journal of Researches* and, again, in 1905 under the title *The Voyage of the "Beagle"*.

Why Am I a Slave?

Frederick Douglass

Why am I a slave? I will run away. I will not stand it. Get caught, or get clear, I'll try it. I had as well die with ague as the fever. I have only one life to lose. I had as well be killed running as die standing. Only think of it; one hundred miles straight north, and I am free![44]

ço ٍç

Frederick Douglass (c.1818-1895) escaped from slavery in 1838. Soon, he had become a leading activist, author and public speaker in the abolitionist movement. Famously, he argued that free speech was society's "great moral renovator." As he put it,

No right was deemed by the fathers of the Government more sacred than the right of speech. It was in their eyes, as in the eyes of all thoughtful men, the great moral renovator of society and government ... Liberty is meaningless where the right to utter one's thoughts and opinions has ceased to exist. That, of all rights, is the dread of tyrants.[45]

The son of a black slave, Harriet Bailey, and a white father, most likely his mother's owner, he abandoned his birth name, Frederick Augustus Washington Bailey, hoping that the name Douglass (taken from Scott's hero in *The Lady of the Lake*) would help him avoid recapture.[46] From 1845 to 1847, he visited England and Ireland, returning to the United States only after some of his English friends had purchased his freedom for him.

During the American Civil War, Douglass assisted in the recruiting of freemen and newly liberated slaves for the 54th and 55th Massachusetts Regiments of the Union Army, imploring "the imperiled nation to unchain against her foes, her powerful black hand."[47] Following the *Emancipation Proclamation* of 1862 and the end of the war in 1865, he was appointed the United States Minister to Haiti. In 1877, he became the first Black US Marshal. Two years after the death of his first wife Anna Murray-Douglass, Douglass married Helen Pitts, a white suffragist twenty years his junior whose father had been active as part of the pre-Civil War Underground Railroad.

Douglass's several autobiographical volumes include *Narrative of the Life of Frederick Douglass, An American Slave* (1845), *My Bondage and My Freedom* (1857) and *Life and Times of Frederick Douglass* (1892).

Are Women Persons?

Susan B. Anthony

The only question left to be settled now is: Are women persons? I scarcely believe any of our opponents will have the hardihood to say they are not. Being persons, then, women are citizens, and no State has a right to make any new law, or to enforce any old law, which shall abridge their privileges or immunities. Hence, every discrimination against women in the constitutions and laws of the several States is today null and void, precisely as is every one against negroes.[48]

℘ ℘

The most famous of the American suffragettes, Susan B. Anthony (1820-1906) is still often remembered as the "mother of us all." Throughout the 19th century she lobbied, first for the abolition of slavery and, later, for the acknowledgement of women's civil rights, especially the right to vote. In 1872, she was arrested for voting illegally in that year's American presidential election in her hometown of Rochester, New York. She was convicted the following year and fined $100, a fine she refused to pay. She wasn't pardoned until 2020.

In 1878 together with Elizabeth Cady Stanton, Anthony presented Congress with a draft amendment giving women the right to vote. Introduced on the floor of the Senate by Senator Aaron Sargent (R-CA), the amendment became known colloquially as the Susan B. Anthony Amendment. In 1920, it was ratified and became the Nineteenth Amendment to the *Constitution of the United States*.

Since then, various attempts have been made to extend the idea of personhood even further. Many governments now recognize corporations as non-natural persons and, in 2017, the New Zealand parliament became the first government to pass legislation declaring an environmental entity, the Whanganui River, a legal person.[49] Unlike in the case of a corporation, some argue that it is unclear exactly who should have the right to speak on behalf of this new kind of legal entity. Others suggest that without connecting the idea of a person to that of a conscious agent, it is also unclear exactly what could constitute personhood in any future legal decisions.

In 1979, Anthony became the first woman to be depicted on US currency.

Why Are Some Traits Dominant and Some Recessive?

Gregor Mendel

That, so far, no generally applicable law governing the formation and development of hybrids has been successfully formulated can hardly be wondered at by anyone who is acquainted with the extent of the task, and can appreciate the difficulties with which experiments of this class have to contend. ... It requires indeed some courage to undertake a labour of such far-reaching extent; this appears, however, to be the only right way by which we can finally reach the solution of a question the importance of which cannot be overestimated in connection with the history of the evolution of organic forms.[50]

ᔅ ᕒ

Because of his study of the inheritance of various traits in peas, Gregor Mendel (1822-84) postulated a series of genetic laws. It is from these laws that the modern science of genetics was born. By carefully recording characteristics such as plant height and the colour and shape of a plant's seeds, Mendel noticed that some characteristics were regularly passed on to plant offspring while others reappeared only in future generations according to various predictable ratios. As Mendel writes,

The striking regularity with which the same hybrid forms always reappeared whenever fertilization between like species took place suggested further experiments whose task it was to follow the development of hybrids in their progeny.[51]

This work allowed Mendel to introduce a distinction between traits that are dominant and traits that are recessive. It also led him to establish many of the rules of heredity that are today referred to as the Laws of Mendelian Inheritance. In 1866, he published the results of his studies, hypothesizing that invisible factors – now called genes – played a role determining the future characteristics of an organism.

While a student at the University of Vienna, Mendel often tutored other students to make ends meet. Even so, he twice failed his teaching-certificate examination. He also suffered from bouts of depression, leading him to temporarily abandon his studies. Named Johann Mendel by his parents, he changed his name to Gregor when he entered religious life. It was in his monastery that he established the garden where he conducted his famous experiments. Eventually he was elected abbot of his monastery.

In 2000, the Gregor Mendel Institute of Molecular Plant Biology was founded in Vienna, Austria.

Can Any Map Be Coloured Using Just Four Colours?

Francis Guthrie

A student of mine asked me today to give him a reason for a fact which I did not know was a fact – and do not yet. He says that if a figure be any how divided and the compartments differently colored so that figures with any portion of common boundary line are differently colored – four colors may be wanted but not more – the following is his case in which four colors are wanted. Query: cannot a necessity for five or more be invented?[52]

ഇം ൙

The above description of Francis Guthrie's question was written in 1852 by the famous British mathematician Augustus De Morgan. Guthrie (1831-99) and his brother Frederick both studied under De Morgan at University College London. Upon graduation, Francis returned to South Africa where he eventually was appointed professor of mathematics at what was later to become the founding college of the University of Cape Town.

The question of how many colours it takes to colour a map so that no two adjacent regions have the same colour remained an open problem until 1976 when it became the first major mathematical theorem to be proved by computer. Because the Appel-Haken proof (named after Kenneth Appel and Wolfgang Haken) involved so many different cases, the proof is unable to be checked by hand. Since then, other computer-assisted proofs have produced similar, confirming results. Even so, the proofs have not been universally accepted, since no single person will ever be able to work through the accuracy of even one of the proofs in its entirety.

Most computer proofs in mathematics use proofs by exhaustion, proofs that examine a large but finite number of cases that together prove a more general theorem. Such proofs can be controversial since they replace proofs that can be examined step-by-step for their logical accuracy with proofs that rely on computer processes and based only on the empirical reliability of a computer's hardware and software.

Defenders of such proofs argue that the reliability of computer hardware and software can itself be tested more easily and accurately than many human cognitive processes. Even so, critics point out that the emerging field of experimental mathematics, even if reliable, still lacks the kind of mathematical elegance found in most previous proofs. As a result, such proofs fail to provide mathematicians with the kinds of new insights and new mathematical concepts that help human beings understand the mathematical results being proposed.

In short, in what sense does a computer proof advance knowledge if no one understands it?

Is God Dead?

Friedrich Nietzsche

God is dead! God remains dead! And we have killed him! How can we console ourselves, the murderers of all murderers? The holiest and the mightiest thing the world has ever possessed has bled to death under our knives: who will wipe this blood from us? With what water could we clean ourselves? What festivals of atonement, what holy games will we have to invent for ourselves? Is the magnitude of this deed too great for us? Do we not ourselves have to become gods merely to appear worthy of it?[53]

೪ ⌘

Although trained as a philologist, Friedrich Nietzsche (1844-1900) is remembered today more for his novels and his philosophy than for his work in linguistics. His character's famous remark that God is dead is often interpreted to mean that the rise of science and the increasing secularization of Europe is bound to lead to the eventual decline of Western culture. Without religion, it is supposed, we will have nothing to substitute in place of God but ourselves, something that will lead almost certainly to nihilism, the rejection of objective moral values altogether. The suggestion is perhaps more speculative than demonstrative, despite Nietzsche's evocative turn of phrase.

In 1869, Nietzsche was appointed a professor of philology at the age of just twenty-four. He resigned a decade later due to ill health. Legend has it that ten years later he saw a horse being beaten in the street. Stepping in to defend the animal, he wrapped his arms around its neck while weeping. Shortly afterward, he suffered a mental breakdown.

Upon his death, Nietzsche's sister Elisabeth became his literary executor. Scholars argue over the extent to which her close association with fascism may have led to Nietzsche's writings being used in the promotion of Nazi causes. What is known is that during the First World War, German soldiers at the front were given copies of *Thus Spoke Zarathustra*, in which Nietzsche describes the rise of the *übermensch*, a master race that is destined to rule the world. Later, during the Second World War, the Nazis claimed Nietzsche's master-slave morality as one of their inspirations, using it to help justify some of the worst brutalities and atrocities in human history.

On May 10, 1933, just a few months after the Nazis gained power in Germany, some 40,000 spectators gathered to watch 20,000 books being burned in an open square next to the University of Berlin. Similar book burnings were held that same night at over thirty German universities.[54] Unlike the writings of Albert Einstein, Sigmund Freud, Helen Keller, H.G. Wells, Émile Zola, Marcel Proust, Bertolt Brecht, Ernest Hemingway, Jack London, Thomas Mann and many others, Nietzsche's books were not among those being consigned to the flames.

Is There Just One Size of Infinity?

Georg Cantor

Take the collection of all positive whole numbers n and denote it by (n); further, imagine the collection of all positive real numbers x and denote it by (x); the question is simply whether (n) and (x) can be corresponded so that each individual of one collection corresponds to one and only one individual of the other.[55]

ॐ ॐ

The above question was first asked by Georg Cantor (1845-1918) in correspondence with the mathematician Richard Dedekind on November 29, 1873. The question opened the door to the first major advances in studying the infinite since the time of Aristotle. By showing that it is impossible to place the members of some infinite sets (or collections) in one-to-one correspondence with each other, Cantor showed that, if even one infinite set exists, then there must exist infinitely many different sizes of infinity.

The main theorem bearing his name, Cantor's Theorem, states that for any set, S, the set of all subsets of S (also called the power set of S) has a size (or cardinality) strictly greater than that of S itself. The theorem is elementary in the finite case but surprising in the infinite case. Before the result was proved, it was generally assumed that all infinite collections had to be equinumerous.

A promising violinist as a young man, Cantor received his doctorate at the age of just twenty-two and was appointed a full professor at the University of Halle at just thirty-four. His theorem was contentious, with his former mathematics professor Leopold Kronecker attacking Cantor as a "scientific charlatan" and a "corrupter of youth,"[56] and with the philosopher Ludwig Wittgenstein calling Cantor's result "utter nonsense."[57] The attacks appear to have been a factor in Cantor's numerous periods of depression, some of which led to his hospitalization.

In contrast, the great 19th-century mathematician David Hilbert summed up the views of most set theorists when he remarked, "No one shall expel us from the paradise that Cantor has created."[58]

Why Do We Dream?

Sigmund Freud

"But what occurrence gave rise to this dream?" I ask. "You know that the stimulus of a dream always lies among the experiences of the preceding day."[59]

ço ও

Founder of the psychoanalytic school of psychology, Sigmund Freud (1856-1939) postulated several ideas that have been influential for the study of the mind. These include the prominence of sexual desire in explaining large portions of human behaviour, the postulation of an unconscious mind, and the division of the human mind into an id (the source of our uncoordinated, instinctual desires), a super-ego (the source of our critical and moralizing faculties), and an ego (the agent that mediates between the id and super-ego).

In his book *The Interpretation of Dreams*, Freud defends a wish-fulfillment theory of dreams in which we *dream about* what we *dream of*, suggesting that dreams find their basis in the conscious desires of the waking mind. Many ordinary desires then appear in our dreams in straightforward ways. Other, less acceptable desires (often relating to sex), appear in unrecognizable ways that can be decoded only with the help of a psychoanalyst. Despite the theory's early renown, it is now rejected by most modern dream theorists.

After graduating with a degree in medicine at the University of Vienna in 1881 and with his habilitation in 1885,

Freud established a clinical practice in Vienna in 1886. His publications included not only his scientific work, but also articles celebrating the effects of cocaine, something he later abandoned, saying that its use proved too much of a distraction from his work. Despite being nominated for a Nobel prize thirteen times, he never won.

With the rise of Nazism, Freud fled Germany in 1938 to avoid persecution, remarking, "What progress we are making. In the Middle Ages they would have burnt me; nowadays they are content with burning my books."[60] He died in London a year later at the age of eighty-three.

What Causes Radioactivity?

Marie Curie

It was at the close of the year 1897 that I began to study the compounds of uranium, the properties of which had greatly attracted my interest. Here was a substance emitting spontaneously and continuously radiations similar to Roentgen rays, whereas ordinarily Roentgen rays can be produced only in a vacuum-tube with the expenditure of energy. By what process can uranium furnish the same rays without expenditure of energy and without undergoing apparent modification? Is uranium the only body whose compounds emit similar rays? Such were the questions I asked myself, and it was while seeking to answer them that I entered into the researches which have led to the discovery of radium.[61]

ை ஒ

Born in Warsaw, Poland, and christened Maria Salomea Skłodowska, Marie Curie (1867-1934) studied at Warsaw's clandestine Flying University, an underground educational institution established to avoid government censorship at a time when Poland was still a part of the Russian Empire.

Later, Curie followed her sister to study in Paris where she eventually became the first woman to receive a PhD from a French university. In 1903 for their research on radioactivity, Curie and her husband Pierre were awarded the Nobel Prize in Physics. Together, the Curies had processed tons of ore to isolate small amounts of uranium and other radioactive elements.

In 1906, Marie was appointed Professor of Physics at the Sorbonne, the same year that Pierre died. In 1911, she became the first person to receive a second Nobel Prize when she received the Nobel Prize in Chemistry for the discovery of the two new elements, radium and polonium. This same year, she met Albert Einstein at the historic, invitation-only Solvay Conference in Brussels. Meeting on the theme "Radiation and the Quanta," the conference was the first of what would become an ongoing series of conferences relating to work being done in both physics and chemistry.

During the First World War, Curie provided medical aid to wounded French soldiers and in 1935 her daughter Irène Joliot-Curie and her son-in-law Frédéric Joliot-Curie were also jointly awarded a Nobel prize for Chemistry. It is to Curie that we owe the term "radioactivity".

How High Can We Build?

John Raskob

Bill, how high can you make it so that it won't fall down?[62]

჎ ჎

John Raskob (1879-1950) was the builder and original owner of New York City's Empire State Building. Completed in 1931 at the beginning of the Great Depression, the building was known for many years as the *Empty* State Building. It didn't begin to turn a profit until the end of the Second World War, shortly after it was hit by a B-25 bomber in 1945. Flying in thick fog, the bomber hit the building between the 78th and 80th floors and caused the death of the pilot, two other crewmen and eleven office workers. The building remained the world's tallest office tower for over forty years.

Raskob addressed his question about the potential height of the building to the building's architect, William Lamb. After studying at the École des Beaux-Arts in Paris, as well as at Williams College and Columbia University, Lamb was involved in the construction of many of New York's most notable, early 20th-century buildings. In the lead-up to the 1939 New York World's Fair, he also served as Coordinator of Design for the Fair's Board of Planners. In answer to Raskob's question, Lamb and his colleagues designed a building that stands 1,250 feet (381.0 metres) to the roof line and 1,454 feet (443.2 metres) to the tip of the building's tower.

Today, the Burj Khalifa in Dubai in the United Arab Emirates holds the record for being the world's tallest building (and the world's tallest structure) at 2,722 feet (829.8 metres), or just over half a mile. The Merdeka 118 in Kuala Lumpur in Malaysia, standing at 2,227 feet (678.9 metres), is the second tallest. The Warsaw Radio Mast, standing at 2,121 feet (646.4 metres) in Poland, is the tallest guyed mast. The CN Tower, at a height of 1,815.3 feet (553.3 metres) in Toronto, remains the tallest freestanding structure in the Western Hemisphere.

What Would It Be Like To Travel at the Speed of Light?

Albert Einstein

During that year [between October 1895 and October 1896, when Einstein was 16] in Aarau [where Einstein attended high school] the question came to me: If one runs after a light wave with [a velocity equal to] light velocity, then one would encounter a time-independent wavefield. However, something like that does not seem to exist! This was the first juvenile thought experiment which has to do with the special theory of relativity.[63]

ی‌ ﭐ

In 1905, Albert Einstein (1879-1955) published his special theory of relativity, arguing that Galileo's principle of relativity – that all uniform motion is relative – can be generalized from simple classical mechanics to all physical phenomena, including electrodynamics. His general theory of relativity, which identifies gravity with a geometric property of spacetime, followed eleven years later. Both theories became famous, not only for their scientific importance but also because of their many counterintuitive consequences. Today, both the special theory and the general theory are among the most highly confirmed theories in the history of science.

Born in Ulm in the Kingdom of Württemberg in the German Empire in 1879, Einstein excelled at mathematics, physics, philosophy and music. With his family's approval, he renounced his German citizenship at the age of sixteen to avoid military service so he could continue his academic studies in Switzerland. After graduating from the Federal Polytechnic in Zurich in 1900, he began work at the Swiss Patent Office in Bern where he reviewed patent applications for a variety of technical, mechanical and scientific devices. In 1902, he and his friends began a discussion group to study the work of mathematicians and philosophers such as Ernst Mach, Henri Poincaré and David Hume. He received his PhD from the University of Zurich in 1905. In 1908, he was appointed lecturer and, in 1909, he became an associate professor at the University of Bern. Later, he accepted a position at the Humbolt University of Berlin and once again became a German citizen.

In 1933 while travelling abroad, Einstein learned that he and other Jewish intellectuals were being forced to give up their teaching positions at German universities. Once again, he renounced his citizenship. Arriving in England, he asked Churchill to help rescue Jewish scientists from Germany. Believing it would help with the war effort, Churchill did what he could to begin placing them in British universities.

In Germany, book burnings began to include Einstein's works and a bounty was placed on Einstein's head. After accepting an offer to join the Institute for Advanced Study at Princeton University, Einstein became an American citizen in 1940.

How Can There Be Peace?

Lester Pearson

How can there be peace without people understanding each other; and how can this be if they don't know each other?[64]

ઝ ૅ

The 1956 Suez Crisis was a military and diplomatic confrontation in Egypt that threatened to divide the United States, France, Great Britain and other western powers, potentially leading to a dissolution of the Western military alliance that had brought an end to the Second World War. In his role as President of the 7th Session of the United Nations General Assembly, future Canadian Prime Minister Lester Pearson (1897-1972) spear-headed the idea of introducing the UN's first large-scale, armoured, peacekeeping force to help resolve the crisis. On 4 November 1956, members of the United Nations voted in favour of the idea and soon afterwards the United Nations Emergency Force, under the command of Canadian General E.L.M. Burns, was employed.

A talented diplomat noted for his suggestions that "Politics is the skilled use of blunt objects"[65] and that "Diplomacy is letting someone else have your way,"[66] Pearson served with the Canadian Army Medical Corps during the First World War. Later, he was transferred to Britain's Royal Flying Corps where he served as a flying officer and where a flight instructor began calling him "Mike", thinking that "Lester" wasn't a masculine enough name for a pilot. The nickname stuck with him for the rest of his life. Although he survived an airplane crash during training, he was discharged from duty only after being hit by a bus in London during a citywide blackout. After receiving degrees from the University of Toronto and the University of Oxford, Pearson eventually was appointed Canada's ambassador to the United States. Later he became Secretary of State for External Affairs. After serving as President of the United Nations General Assembly, he served as Leader of the Official Opposition from 1958 to 1963 and as Prime Minister of Canada from 1963 to 1968.

In 1958, Pearson was awarded the Nobel Peace Prize for his role in helping to end the Suez Crisis. Today, over 100,000 peacekeepers are deployed around the world.

Who Plans Best?

Friedrich Hayek

> This is not a dispute about whether planning is to be done or
> not. It is a dispute as to whether planning is to be done
> centrally, by one authority for the whole economic system, or
> is to be divided among many individuals.[67]

ဆုန်

To be successful, planning – especially economic planning –
needs to be based on knowledge. The successful allocation of
resources, especially scarce resources, needs to be based on a
large number of factors, not the least of which are people's
individual preferences. But as Friedrich Hayek (1899-1992)
points out, the more distant the planner is from these
preferences, the less likely planning will be successful. In
Hayek's words,

> In any society in which many people collaborate, this
> planning, whoever does it, will in some measure have to be
> based on knowledge which, in the first instance, is not given to
> the planner but to somebody else, which somehow will have to
> be conveyed to the planner.[68]

How this knowledge is to be communicated "is the crucial
problem for any theory explaining the economic process, and
the problem of what is the best way of utilizing knowledge
initially dispersed among all the people is at least one of the

59

main problems of economic policy – or of designing an efficient economic system."[69] It was in part for this insight that Hayek was awarded the Nobel Prize in Economics in 1974.

Born in Vienna, Hayek earned doctoral degrees in both law and political science. After the First World War, Hayek began studying economics, in part because he was troubled by the poverty of post-war Europe. Like others, he hoped that an improved understanding of economics would help provide a key to improved living conditions in the post-war period.[70] He became a British citizen in 1938 and spent most of his working life at the London School of Economics, the University of Chicago and the University of Freiburg.

In 1991, Hayek was awarded the Presidential Medal of Freedom from President George H.W. Bush. In 2011, his 1945 article "The Use of Knowledge in Society" was chosen as one of the top twenty articles published in the *American Economic Review* during its first century of publication. His most influential books include *The Road to Serfdom* (1944), *Individualism and Economic Order* (1948) and *The Constitution of Liberty* (1960).

Is Adolescence Always an Unhappy Time?

Margaret Mead

I have tried to answer the question which sent me to Samoa:
Are the disturbances which vex our adolescents due to the
nature of adolescence itself or to the civilization? Under
different conditions does adolescence present a different
picture?[71]

ల ∞

After interviewing 68 young Samoan women between the ages
of nine and twenty, Margaret Mead (1901-1978) famously but
controversially concluded that the emotional and psychological distresses that often accompany the passage from childhood to adulthood are due more to cultural factors (such as
prohibitions on premarital sex) than to physical factors (such
as the onset of puberty). Her research was contentious since
she failed to apply many of the now-standard research
protocols believed necessary for obtaining reliable results in
the social sciences. Even so, as one of the first modern cultural
anthropologists to be involved in cross-cultural studies,
Mead's influence was enormous and her work helped usher in
the 1960s sexual revolution.

A student of Franz Boas (who has often been called the
"father of American anthropology"), and of Ruth Benedict (a
future president of the American Anthropological Association
and with whom Mead later had an intimate relationship), Mead
received her PhD from Columbia University in 1929. In 1944,

she founded the Institute for Intercultural Studies, an institute that worked to advance knowledge of intercultural understanding and international relations.

In 1975, Mead was appointed President of the American Association for the Advancement of Science and, in 1979, she was posthumously awarded the Presidential Medal of Freedom by President Jimmy Carter. Her most notable books include *Coming of Age in Somoa* (1928), *Male and Female* (1949) and *Growth and Culture* (1951).

Today, Mead is often remembered for her comment that "A small group of thoughtful people could change the world. Indeed, it's the only thing that ever has."[72]

Is It Better To Have
Freedom from or *Freedom to*?

Isaiah Berlin

For it is this, the 'positive' conception of liberty: not freedom from, but freedom to – to lead one prescribed form of life – which the adherents of the 'negative' notion represent as being, at times, no better than a specious disguise for brutal tyranny.[73]

ço cò

Born in Riga, Latvia, Isaiah Berlin (1909-97) moved with his family to Britain in 1921. Except for his time working for the British Diplomatic Service during the Second World War, he spent all his adult life at the University of Oxford. In 1946 he was appointed a Commander of the British Empire. In 1957 he was knighted and in 1971 he received the Order of Merit. From 1965 to 1975 he served as founding President of Wolfson College. From 1974 to 1978 he served as President of the British Academy. Oxford's annual Isaiah Berlin Lecture is named in his honour.

Remembered for his defence of value pluralism as well as for his opposition to Marxism and communism, Berlin's most famous lecture, "Two Concepts of Liberty," was delivered at Oxford in 1958. In it, Berlin defined *negative liberty* as the absence of coercion, the absence of interference with a person's actions. He defined *positive liberty* as the power to act using one's free will to achieve one's own desired ends.

Both types of liberty are important. As Berlin notes, since "Freedom for the wolves has often meant death to the sheep,"[74] complete positive liberty can hardly be thought an ideal social good. At the same time, too much restraint, even if dressed up in the guise of benevolence, is not much better. As Berlin notes,

> to manipulate men, to propel them toward goals which you – the social reformers – see, but they may not, is to deny their human essence, to treat them as objects without wills of their own and therefore to degrade them.[75]

Put another way, "Liberty is liberty, not equality or fairness or justice or culture, or human happiness or a quiet conscience."[76] Instead, it is "an inalienable ingredient in what makes human beings human."[77]

This understanding of the importance of human liberty was linked to Berlin's theory of value pluralism:

> If, as I believe, the ends of men are many, and not all of them are in principle compatible with each other, then the possibility of conflict – and of tragedy – can never wholly be eliminated from human life, either personal or social.[78]

Even though it is true that "Out of the crooked timber of humanity, nothing completely straight was ever made,"[79] the ability for each of us to try and sometimes fail is still part of what makes a good life. It is for this reason that we all need to recognize that "Utopias have their value – nothing so wonderfully expands the imaginative horizons of human potentialities – but as guides to conduct they can prove literally fatal."[80]

❦ ❧

Can Machines Think?

Alan Turing

I propose to consider the question, "Can machines think?"[81]

୨୦ ଏଙ

During the Second World War, Alan Turing (1912-1954) worked as a code breaker at Britain's famous Bletchley Park. As head of Hut 8, the section responsible for breaking Germany's naval codes, Turing played a crucial role in helping achieve the Allied victory. His work helped the Allies decode German naval messages that had been encrypted using the famous Enigma coding machine, something that helped shorten the war and save thousands of lives.

In 1950, Turing launched the modern study of artificial intelligence with his famous article, "Computing Machinery and Intelligence." Because he was the first to formalize the idea of an algorithm in a way that was applicable to the development of the modern, electronic computer, he sometimes is referred to as the "father of computer science."

In 1952, after having an affair with a nineteen-year-old Manchester man, he was convicted of gross indecency and sentenced to chemical castration. The conviction meant that he also lost his security clearance. He committed suicide two years later.

In 2013, Turing received a posthumous royal pardon under the Royal Prerogative of Mercy. As the British Justice Minister commented at the time, Turing's "later life was overshadowed by his conviction for homosexual activity, a sentence we would now consider unjust and discriminatory and which has now been repealed." He "deserves to be remembered and recognised for his fantastic contribution to the war effort and his legacy to science. A pardon from the Queen is a fitting tribute to an exceptional man."[82]

In 2017, the British government also passed the "Alan Turing Law," granting retroactive pardons to all others who had been similarly convicted. The story of Turing's life, including his work as a code breaker, is told in the film *The Imitation Game*, based on a biography of Turing written by Andrew Hodges.

Are We Alone?

Arthur C. Clarke

Two possibilities exist: either we are alone in the Universe or
we are not. Both are equally terrifying.[83]

ৎৡ ৯৶

Arthur C. Clarke (1917-2008) was an English science-fiction
writer and futurist, famous in part for co-writing the
screenplay for the 1968 film *2001: A Space Odyssey*. In the
film, astronauts discover an alien monolith on the surface of
the moon and an even larger monolith orbiting the planet
Jupiter. Together with their lifelike but unreliable super-
computer HAL, they go in search of extra-terrestrial life. As
Clarke points out – and as viewers are reminded in the film –
both the possibility that we are alone in the universe and the
possibility that we are not can seem terrifying, each in its own
way.

In 1979, Gordon Walker and his colleagues at the
University of British Columbia were the first to detect an
extrasolar planet. (The term is now commonly shortened to
"exoplanet.") Even so, it took significant advances in both
theory and technology for scientists to be confident that this
was in fact what had been observed. It wasn't until 1995 when
two other scientists, Michel Mayor and Didier Queloz at the
University of Geneva, produced less ambiguous results that
the astronomical world became convinced that exoplanets

orbiting solar-type stars in fact existed. In 2019, Mayor and Queloz were awarded a Nobel Prize for their discovery.[84]

Today, two main methods are used to confirm the existence of exoplanets. The first is the *doppler spectroscopy* (or *wobble*) *method*, in which astronomers look for small doppler shifts in the spectrum of a planet's parent star. In school, we are taught that planets revolve around the sun, but this isn't quite correct. Instead, the sun and planets together revolve around the centre of mass of the entire solar system, which is close but not identical to the centre of the sun. As the sun moves, its light shifts slightly, depending on whether it is moving toward or away from an observer. By studying these shifts, astronomers are able to calculate the gravitational influences of a sun's orbiting planets.

The second method is the *transit method*, in which astronomers measure small changes in a star's brightness as a planet crosses (or transits) in front of it. In just a few decades, scientists have used these two methods to discover over 3,800 exoplanets, as well as thousands of other planet candidates observed in just a fraction of the known universe.

Do any of these planets have the kind of environment that would support life? And if so, is it likely that we one day will be able to communicate with other life forms? On the one hand, the enormous size of the known universe and the huge number of potential exoplanets might lead us to think that the possibility of there existing extraterrestrial life must be extremely high. On the other hand, the enormous distances in time and space between stars and galaxies, in which travel at even the speed of light may take thousands if not millions of years, will almost guarantee that communication between alien civilizations will be unlikely.

Are Human Beings Inherently Evil?

Nelson Mandela

Are human beings inherently evil? What infuses individuals with the ego and ambition to so clamour for power that genocide assumes the mantle of means that justify coveted ends?[85]

ço eç

Given a life sentence for his opposition to South Africa's system of institutional racial segregation known as apartheid, Nelson Mandela (1918-2013) served 27 years in prison before being released in 1990. At the time, the *Population Registration Act* classified all South Africans into four racial categories: Black, White, Coloured and Indian. Other acts prohibited interracial marriage and restricted the ownership of land, the place of residence and the voting rights of the majority of South Africa's citizens.

In 1979 while still in prison, Mandela was taken to hospital for a small injury. While there he "sensed a thawing" in relations between black and white South Africans:

> The doctor and nurses had treated me in a natural way as though they had been dealing with blacks on a basis of equality all their lives. This was something new and different to me, and an encouraging sign. It reaffirmed my long-held belief that education was the enemy of prejudice. These were men and women of science, and science had no room for racism.[86]

In 1991 after being released from prison, Mandela was elected president of the African National Congress (ANC), the leading anti-apartheid political movement at the time. Prior to Mandela's release, the ANC like many other political movements had been outlawed.

Three years later, Mandela became the first democratically elected President of South Africa. Together with Archbishop Desmond Tutu and other South African leaders, Mandela then set to work dismantling apartheid and establishing a program of national reconciliation.

Given his unwavering faith in democracy, perhaps it is not surprising that in answer to the question of whether human beings are inherently evil, Mandela remarked as follows:

> I would venture to say that there is something inherently good in all human beings ... And, yes, there is also something inherently bad in all of us, flesh and blood as we are ... From this premise arises the challenge to order our lives and mould our mores in such a way that the good in all of us takes precedence. In other words, we are not passive and hapless souls waiting for manna or the plague from on high. All of us have a role to play in shaping society.[87]

In 1993, Mandela shared the Nobel Peace Prize with his predecessor as president, Willem de Klerk. The award was given "for their work for the peaceful termination of the apartheid regime, and for laying the foundations for a new democratic South Africa."[88]

How Can Robots Be Made Safe?

Isaac Asimov

"We have: One, a robot may not injure a human being or, through inaction, allow a human being to come to harm."

"Right!"

"Two," continued Powell, "a robot must obey the orders given to it by human beings except where such orders would conflict with the First Law."

"Right!"

"And three, a robot must protect its own existence as long as such protection does not conflict with the First or Second Laws."

"Right!"[89]

ഔ ൟ

Today, we not only use computer programs to help solve complex problems, we use them to guide the actions of some of the most complex machines ever built. We also use computer programs to help us *write* computer programs, something that makes it likely that no person will ever have the ability to supervise directly the creation of future generations of robots.

A professor of biochemistry at Boston University, Isaac Asimov (1920-1992) was best known for his many science fiction writings, including his popular *Foundation* series, *Galactic Empire* series, and *Robot* series. Credited with introducing the word "robotics" into the English language, he is also famous for creating the three "laws of robotics," intended to help guarantee the safety of human beings in a world dominated by robots.

Is such domination inevitable? No one knows. But some people are concerned. In the words of the Cambridge scientist Stephen Hawking, "The development of full artificial intelligence could spell the end of the human race."[90] In the words of Tesla boss Elon Musk, artificial intelligence is the "biggest existential threat" facing humankind.[91] Whether they are right and whether Asimov's three laws will ever be implemented remain to be seen.

Where Do We Go From Here?

Martin Luther King, Jr

Some years ago a famous novelist died. Among his papers was found a list of suggested plots for future stories, the most prominently underscored being this one: "A widely separated family inherits a house in which they have to live together." This is the great new problem of mankind. We have inherited a large house, a great "world house" in which we have to live together – black and white, Easterner and Westerner, Gentile and Jew, Catholic and Protestant, Muslim and Hindu – a family unduly separated in ideas, culture and interest, who, because we can never again live apart, must learn somehow to live with each other in peace.[92]

༉ ༈

The 20th-century's most influential American civil rights leader, Martin Luther King, Jr (1929-1968) worked tirelessly for racial equality prior to his assassination in Memphis on April 4, 1968. Named *Time* magazine's Man of the Year in 1963 and winner of the Nobel Peace Prize in 1964, King was also awarded over fifty honorary university degrees. His "Letter from a Birmingham Jail" and his "I Have a Dream" speech remain two of the most influential documents of the 20th century.

As a young man, King attended segregated public schools in Georgia. He graduated from high school when he was fifteen. He received a BA in 1948 from Morehouse College in Atlanta and a BD from Crozer Theological Seminary in

Pennsylvania in 1951. He received his PhD from Boston University in 1955.

Arrested some twenty-nine times because of his protest activities, King was almost killed at a book signing when he was stabbed in the chest with a letter opener. In 1956, his home was bombed. On the street outside, King pleaded to the assembled crowd for non-violence.

Among King's books are *Stride Toward Freedom*, King's 1958 account of the Montgomery bus boycott; *Strength to Love*, a collection of his sermons published in 1963; and *Why We Can't Wait*, his report of the 1963 Birmingham campaign. His 1967 book *Where do We Go From Here?* was the last of King's books to be published during his lifetime.

Many of King's most famous speeches and essays, including his "Letter from a Birmingham Jail," his "I Have a Dream" speech, and his "Nobel Prize Acceptance Speech" are included in Clayborne Carson's 2013 anthology, *The Essential Martin Luther King, Jr.*

Who Do You Think You Are?

Alice Munro

Who do you think you are?[93]

৯৵ ৶৶

An Ontario native, Alice Munro (b. 1931) is often cited as a master of the contemporary short story, a genre she said she adopted since she didn't have time to write a novel. Her collection of short stories *Who do You Think You Are?* focuses on a young woman, Rose, as she moves through her formative years, trying to adapt to changing circumstances. For anyone living in the age of identity, her story is a familiar one. Will she choose to identify herself with her upbringing, with her relationships with men, or perhaps with the past child who told a lie about what she had for breakfast, thinking that a more glamorous meal somehow made her a more glamorous person?

At its heart, the modern age has brought with it, not just a new scientific revolution and the diminishment of religious authority. It has also had at its centre the idea of the individual, the idea that people are not simply a product of their birth or their station in life, but that somehow – we don't really know how – individual liberty gives people the ability to create themselves as they want to be known and remembered. Like Rose, we don't want to live alone, without friends and family and social obligations; but neither do we want others to have the power to define us. Like Rose, we don't want a few simple words spoken by someone else – "Who do you think you are?" – to be powerful enough put us in our place.

After receiving three Canadian Governor General's Literary Awards – for *Dance of the Happy Shades* in 1968, *Who Do You Think You Are?* in 1978 and *The Progress of Love* in 1986 – Munro won the Nobel Prize in Literature in 2013. To mark the occasion, the Royal Canadian Mint issued a commemorative Alice Munro five-dollar coin.

What Else Can You Do for Anyone but Inspire Them?

Bob Dylan

The highest purpose of art is to inspire. What else can you do? What else can you do for anyone but inspire them?[94]

∽ ∾

The purpose of art has been debated since ancient times. Plato seems to have had two theories. The first was that, although science *reports* about things in the world, art *imitates* (or mimics) them. The second was that art, especially good art, works to imitate (or mimic) *ideal goods*, goods like beauty, truth and justice. In both cases, good art need not confine itself simply to reporting ordinary, day-to-day, descriptive truths. Instead, good art helps reveal deeper, more important truths.

Plato's most famous student had a different idea. According to Aristotle, Plato was wrong to think it is the job of both science and art to help us learn about the world. According to Aristotle, the purpose of science is to help us *know*. The purpose of art is to help us *feel*.

Pablo Picasso sides with Plato. In Picasso's telling, "We all know that Art is not truth. Art is a lie that makes us realize truth."[95]

Bob Dylan (b.1941) sides with Aristotle. Good art, good music and good poetry don't *describe*. Instead, according to Dylan they *inspire*.

Dylan's most celebrated works appeared in the 1960s, when songs such as "Blowin' in the Wind" and "The Times They are a-Changin'" helped inspire a generation committed to the civil rights and anti-war movements. When he signed his first record contract with Columbia, he told the company's representative that he was an orphan so he could get around the requirement that his parents would have to co-sign the contract with him.

In 2015, *Rolling Stone* ranked Dylan as the number-one songwriter of all time. A year later, he was awarded the Nobel Prize in Literature. Such recognition is not bad for a guy who says he once traded an Elvis Presley painting by Andy Warhol for a sofa.[96]

Acknowledgements

As the British Prime Minister Benjamin Disraeli once said, "I feel a very unusual sensation. If it is not indigestion, I think it must be gratitude."[97]

In my case, the gratitude I feel makes it necessary for me to extend a sincere and affectionate thank you to all my students. Over many decades, you have made teaching a pleasure. You have also made it easy to remember just how invigorating life at university can be for young and old alike.

Thank you all.

A. Troglodyte

Notes

† The motto *Sapere aude* (or *Dare to know*) was introduced by the Roman poet Horace in his *First Book of Letters* some two thousand years ago. In 1784, the philosopher Immanuel Kant re-introduced the phrase in his essay *What is Enlightenment?,* using it as a motto for the entire Age of Enlightenment. In both cases, the slogan was meant to remind readers that reason is something that can guide us profitably in all areas of human activity.

[1] Homer, *Iliad, Books 1-12* (Loeb Classical Library, Homer, vol. 1), translated by A.T. Murray and William F. Wyatt, 2nd edn, Cambridge (MA), London: Harvard University Press, bk 9, 337-41, 1999, p. 419.

[2] Plato, *The Republic*, bk 2, 357a, in Plato, *Complete Works*, edited by John M. Cooper and D.S. Hutchinson, Indianapolis: Hackett Publishing Company, 1997, p. 998.

[3] Aristotle, *Topics*, 1, 100a25-30, in Aristotle, *The Complete Works of Aristotle*, 2 vols, edited by Jonathan Barnes, Princeton: Princeton University Press, 1984, vol. 1, p. 167.

[4] Aristotle, quoted in Christopher Shields, "Aristotle," *Stanford Encyclopedia of Philosophy* (Spring 2022 edn), 2020, sec. 1, plato.stanford.edu/entries/aristotle/.

[5] Leonardo da Vinci, *Codex Leicester*, 4r, in Leonardo da Vinci, *The Notebooks of Leonardo Da Vinci*, edited by Edward MacCurdy, 2 vols, New York: Reynal & Hitchcock, [no date], vol. 1, p. 418.

[6] Elizabeth Abbott, quoted in "Da Vinci's Sex Life Reveals a Complex Understanding of Male Love," *CBC Radio*, 28 January 2020, www.cbc.ca/radio/ideas/da-vinci-s-sex-life-reveals-a-complex-understanding-of-male-love-1.5442235.

[7] Sigmund Freud, *Leonardo Da Vinci: A Memory of His Childhood*, London: Arc Paperbacks, 1984, p. 72.

[8] Niccolò Machiavelli, *The Prince* [1532], translated by George Bull, Harmondsworth (UK): Penguin Books, 1981, ch. 17, p. 96.

[9] The character Hamlet, in William Shakespeare, *Hamlet*, act 3, scene 1, in William Shakespeare, *The Annotated Shakespeare*, 3 vols, edited by A.L. Rowse, New York: Clarkson N. Potter, Inc., 1978, vol. 3, p. 225.

[10] *Ibid.*, act 2, scene 2.

[11] *Ibid.*

[12] Bill Bryson, *Shakespeare: The World as Stage*, New York: Atlas Books, 2007, p. 113.

[13] Pamela Hill Nettleton, *William Shakespeare: Playwright and Poet*, Minneapolis: Capstone, 2008, p. 89.

[14] Ben Jonson, quoted in Jonathan Bate, *Soul of the Age: A Biography of the Mind of William Shakespeare*, New York: Random House, 2009, p. xvii.

[15] "The Abjuration of Galileo Galilei of 22 June 1633 in Front of the Inquisition," in Maurice A. Finocchiaro (ed.), *The Galileo Affair: A Documentary History*, Berkeley: University of California Press, 1989, p. 292.

[16] *Address by Pope John Paul II to the Participants in the Plenary Session of the Pontifical Academy of Sciences*, 31 October 1992, www.vatican.va/content/john-paul-ii/it/speeches/1992/october/documents/hf_jp-ii_spe_19921031_accademia-scienze.html.

[17] Thomas Hobbes, *Leviathan Parts I and II* [1651], edited by A.P. Martinich, Peterborough, ON: Broadview Editions, 2005, pt 1, ch. 13, para., 8, 19, pp. 95-96.

[18] Thomas Hobbes, quoted in Bernard Gert, *Hobbes,* Cambridge UK, Malden USA: Polity, 2010, ch. 1.

[19] Thomas Hobbes, *Leviathan Parts I and II* [1651], edited by A.P. Martinich, Peterborough, ON: Broadview Editions, 2005, p. 157.

[20] *Ibid.*

[21] Noel Malcolm, "A Summary Biography of Hobbes," in Tom Sorell (ed.) *The Cambridge Companion to Hobbes*, Cambridge: Cambridge University Press, 1996, p. 38. See too Julie E. Cooper, "Thomas Hobbes on the Political Theorist's Vocation," *The Historical Journal*, 50 (2007), p. 543.

[22] John Locke, *Two Treatises of Government* [1690], Indianapolis: Bobbs-Merrill Educational Publishing, 1952, para. 240, p. 138.

[23] John Locke, quoted in Bird T. Baldwin, "John Locke's Contributions to Education," *The Sewanee Review*, 21 (April, 1913), p. 179, www.jstor.org/stable/27532614.

[24] William Stukeley, *Memoirs of Sir Isaac Newton's Life* [1752], London: Taylor and Francis, 1936, pp. 19-20.

[25] Isaac Newton, quoted in E.T. Bell, *Men of Mathematics*, New York Touchstone, 2014, p. 90.

[26] Gottfried Leibniz, "Principles of Nature and Grace, Based on Reason" [1714], §7, in Gottfried Leibniz, *Philosophical Essays*, translated by Roger Ariew and Daniel Garber, Indianapolis: Hackett Publishing Company, 1989, pp. 209-10.

[27] *Ibid.*, p. 210.

[28] Voltaire, *Candide, ou l'Optimisme* [*Candide, or All for the Best*], Geneva: Cramer, 1759.

[29] Jean-Jacques Rousseau, *Du contrat social ou Principes du droit politique* [1762], bk 1, ch. 1, sec. 1, in Jean-Jacques Rousseau, *On the Social Contract*, translated by Donald A. Cress, Indianapolis: Hackett Publishing Company, 1987.

[30] David Wootton, "Introduction," in Jean-Jacques Rousseau, *Basic Political Writings*, 2nd edn, Donald A. Cress (trans.), Indianapolis/Cambridge: Hackett Publishing Company, 2011, p. xiv.

[31] Jean-Jacques Rousseau, *Basic Political Writings*, 2nd edn, Donald A. Cress (trans.), Indianapolis/Cambridge: Hackett Publishing Company, 2011, p. 43.

[32] Jean-Jacques Rousseau, *Du contrat social ou Principes du droit politique* [1762], bk 1, ch. 1, sec. 1, in Jean-Jacques Rousseau, *On the Social Contract*, translated by Donald A. Cress, Indianapolis: Hackett Publishing Company, 1987.

[33] *Ibid.*, bk 1, ch. 1, sec. 7.

[34] Adam Smith, *An Inquiry into the Nature and Causes of the Wealth of Nations* [1776], Chicago: University of Chicago Press, 1976, bk 1, ch. 2, para. 2, p. 19.

[35] *Ibid.*

[36] Adam Smith, quoted in Robert L. Heilbroner, "Legacy of Adam Smith," *Britannica*,
www.britannica.com/biography/Adam-Smith/Legacy.

[37] Heinrich Olbers, "On the Transparency of Space" [1823], in Edward Harrison, *Darkness at Night: A Riddle of the Universe*, Cambridge, MA: Harvard University Press, 1987, p. 224.

[38] Thomas Robert Malthus, *On Population* [1798], New York: The Modern Library, 1960, p. 52.

[39] James Bonar, *Malthus and his Work*, 2nd edn, London: Frank Cass & Co. Ltd,1966, p. 1.

[40] Thomas Robert Malthus, *On Population* [1798], New York: The Modern Library, 1960, p. 9.

[41] *Ibid.*, p. 17.

[42] Charles Darwin, *On the Origin of Species by Means of Natural Selection* [1859], edited by Joseph Carroll, Peterborough, ON: Broadview Press, 2003, p.132.

[43] *Ibid.*, pp.132-3.

[44] Frederick Douglass, *Narrative of the Life of Frederick Douglass, An American Slave*, Boston: The Anti-Slavery Office, 1845, Ch 10.

[45] Frederick Douglass, "Pleas for Free Speech in Boston," Boston, 8 June 1880.

[46] Being able to disappear using a pseudonym is something many people sometimes long for, even when their situations are not nearly so drastic as that of Douglass. When wanting to appear as someone other than A. Troglodyte, I have sometimes published under the name A.D. Irvine.

[47] Frederick Douglass, "Men of Color, To Arms!" Rochester, 21 March 1863.

[48] Susan B. Anthony, "Constitutional Argument, 1872," in Ellen C. DuBois (ed.),*The Elizabeth Cady Stanton – Susan B. Anthony Reader: Correspondence, Writings, Speeches*, rev. edn, Boston: Northeastern University Press, 1992, pp. 157-8.

[49] APNZ, "Agreement Entitles Whanganui River to Legal Identity," *New Zealand Herald*, 29 August 2012, www.nzherald.co.nz/nz/agreement-entitles-whanganui-river-to-legal-identity/VLED2SURDQGJHFREHDBHQZDNHM/.

[50] Gregor Mendel, *Experiments in Plant Hybridization* [1865], New York: Cosimo Classics, 2008, p. 8.

[51] Gregor Mendel, *Gregor Mendel's Experiments on Plant Hybrids*, Alain F. Corcos and Floyd V. Monaghan (eds), New Brunswick, NJ: Rutgers University Press, 1993, p. 59.

[52] Augustus De Morgan, quoted in Robin Wilson, *Four Colors Suffice: How the Map Problem was Solved*, Princeton, NJ: Princeton University Press, 2014, p. 18; cf. Francis Guthrie, "Note on the Coloring of Maps," *Proceedings of the Royal Society of Edinburgh*, 10 (1880), pp. 727-8.

[53] Friedrich Nietzsche, "The Madman," in *The Gay Science* [1882], edited by Bernard Williams, Cambridge (MA), New York: Cambridge University Press, 2001, bk 3, sec. 125, p. 120.

[54] United States Holocaust Memorial Museum, "Book Burning," *Holocaust Encyclopedia*, Washington, DC, encyclopedia.ushmm.org/content/en/article/book-burning.

[55] Georg Cantor quoted in Robert Gray, "Georg Cantor and Transcendental Numbers," *American Mathematical Monthly*, 101 (9) (1994), p. 827. Cf. William B. Ewald, *From Immanuel Kant to David Hilbert: A Source Book in the Foundations of Mathematics, Volume 2*, New York: Oxford University Press, 1996, p. 844.

[56] Leopold Kronecker, quoted in Joseph Dauben, *Georg Cantor: His Mathematics and Philosophy of the Infinite*, Princeton, NJ: Princeton University Press, 1990, p. 1.

[57] Ludwig Wittgenstein, quoted in Victor Rodych, "Wittgenstein's Philosophy of Mathematics," in Edward N. Zalta (ed.), *The Stanford Encyclopedia of Philosophy*, 2007, plato.stanford.edu/entries/wittgenstein-mathematics.

[58] David Hilbert, quoted in Constance Reid, *Hilbert*, New York: Springer-Verlag, 1996, p. 177.

[59] Sigmund Freud, *The Basic Writings of Sigmund Freud*, New York: The Modern Library, 1938, p. 226.

[60] Ruth Sheppard, *Sigmund Freud: The Man, The Scientist, and the Birth of Psychoanalysis*, New York: The Rosen Publishing Group, 2022, p. 119.

[61] Marie Curie, "Radium and Radioactivity," *Century Magazine*, January 1904, pp. 461-466.

[62] John Raskob to architect William Lamb, quoted in Jonathan Goldman, *The Empire State Building Book*, New York: St Martin's Press, 1980, p. 30; reprinted in Harry Dederichs, "Empire State Bldg Still Standing Tall after 50 Years," *Kingman Daily Miner*, 28 April 1981, p. B9.

[63] Albert Einstein, quoted in Abraham Pais, '*Subtle is the Lord ...*': *The Science and the Life of Albert Einstein,* Oxford: Clarendon Press, and New York: Oxford University Press, 1982, p. 131.

[64] Lester B. Pearson, *The Four Faces of Peace and the International Outlook*, Toronto: McClelland and Stewart, 1964, p. 17.

[65] Lester B. Pearson, quoted in John Ransley (ed.), *Chambers Dictionary of Political Biography*, London: W. & R. Chambers Ltd, 1991, p. 345.

[66] Lester B. Pearson, quoted in Michael C. Thomsett and Jean Freestone Thomsett, *War and Conflict Quotations*, Jefferson, NC: McFarland & Company Inc., 2015, p. 32.

[67] Friedrich Hayek, "The Use of Knowledge in Society," *American Economic Review*, 35 (1945), 4 (September); reprinted in Friedrich Hayek, *Individualism and Economic Order,* Chicago: University of Chicago Press, 2012, p. 79.

[68] *Ibid.*, p. 78.

[69] *Ibid.*

[70] Mises Institute, "Friedrich A. Hayek," *Mises Institute*, mises.org/profile/friedrich-hayek.

[71] Margaret Mead, *Coming of Age in Samoa: A Psychological Study of Primitive Youth for Western Civilization* [1928], New York: Harper Perennial Modern Classics, 2001, pp. 6-7.

[72] Margaret Mead, quoted in Olivier Serrat, *Knowledge Solutions*, Singapore: Springer Open, 2017, p. 126.

[73] Isaiah Berlin, *Four Essays on Liberty*, London, Oxford, New York: Oxford University Press, 1969, p. 131.

[74] *Ibid.*, p. xlv.

[75] *Ibid.*, p. 137.

[76] Isaiah Berlin, *The Proper Study of Mankind* [1997], New York: Random House, 2012, p. 197.

[77] Isaiah Berlin, *Four Essays on Liberty*, London, Oxford, New York: Oxford University Press, 1969, p. lx.

[78] *Ibid.*, p. 169.

[79] Isaiah Berlin, *The Crooked Timber of Humanity* [1990], 2nd edn, Princeton, Oxford: Princeton University Press, 2013, quoting Kant on p. 50.

[80] *Ibid.*, p. 15.

[81] A.M. Turing, "Computing Machinery and Intelligence," *Mind*, 59 (1950), p. 433.

[82] BBC, "Royal Pardon for Codebreaker Alan Turing," *BBC News*, 24 December, 2013, www.bbc.com/news/technology-25495315.

[83] Arthur C. Clarke, quoted in Chris Impey, *The Living Cosmos: Our Search for Life in the Universe*, Cambridge: Cambridge University Press, 2011, p. 266.

[84] Joshua N. Winn, "Who Really Discovered the First Exoplanet?" *Scientific American*, 12 November 2019, blogs.scientificamerican.com/observations/who-really-discovered-the-first-exoplanet/#.

[85] Nelson Mandela, Speech in Moria, Zionist Christian Church Easter Conference, 03 April 1994, African National Congress Historical Documents Archive, Johannesburg, South Africa.

[86] Nelson Mandela: *Long Walk to Freedom*, London: Little, Brown and Company, 1994, p. 439.

[87] Nelson Mandela, Speech in Moria, Zionist Christian Church Easter Conference, 03 April 1994, African National Congress Historical Documents Archive, Johannesburg, South Africa.

[88] Irwin Abrams (ed.), *Nobel Lectures, Peace 1991-1995*, Singapore: World Scientific Publishing Co., 1999; repr. as "Nelson Mandela: Facts," *The Nobel Peace Prize 1993*, www.nobelprize.org/prizes/peace/1993/mandela/facts/.

[89] Isaac Asimov, "Runaround" [1942], in *Robot Visions,* New York: A ROC Book / New American Library, 1990, p. 126.

[90] Stephen Hawking, quoted in Rory Cellan-Jones, "Stephen Hawking Warns Artificial Intelligence could End Mankind," *BBC News*, 02 December 2014 www.bbc.com/news/technology-30290540.

[91] Elon Musk, quoted in Mark Ward, "Does Rampant AI Threaten Humanity?" *BBC News*, 02 December 2014, www.bbc.com/news/technology-30293863.

[92] Martin Luther King, *Where do We Go from Here: Chaos or Community?* [1967], Boston: Beacon Press, 2010, p. 177.

[93] Alice Munro, *Who Do You Think You Are?* Toronto: Macmillan of Canada,1978.

[94] Bob Dylan, quoted in Jonathan Cott, "Bob Dylan: The Rolling Stone Interview," *Rolling Stone,* 26 January 1978, www.rollingstone.com/music/music-features/bob-dylan-the-rolling-stone-interview-58625/.

[95] Pablo Picasso, quoted in Marius de Zayas, "Picasso Speaks," in *The Arts,* vol. 3, May 1923, p. 315; reprinted in Alfred Barr, *Picasso: 50 Years of His Art*, New York: Museum of Modern Art, 1946, pp. 270-1.

[96] Canadian Broadcasting Corporation, "75 Little-known Facts about Bob Dylan," *CBC Music*, 13 October 2016,

www.cbc.ca/music/read/75-little-known-facts-about-bobdylan-1.5047071?msclkid=887476f8b6d111ec8a569b9001bcd993.

[97] Evan Esar, *20,000 Quips & Quotes*, New York: Barnes & Noble Books, 1995, p. 358.